I0141205

THE NOBLE ONE CALLED "POINT OF PASSAGE WISDOM", A GREAT VEHICLE SUTRA

BY TONY DUFF AND SERGEY DUDKO
PADMA KARPO TRANSLATION COMMITTEE

Copyright © 2011 Tony Duff. All rights reserved. No portion of this book may be reproduced in any form or by any means, electronic or mechanical, including photography, recording, or by any information storage or retrieval system or technologies now known or later developed, without permission in writing from the publisher.

First edition, February 2011
ISBN paper book: 978-9937-572-58-3
ISBN e-book: 978-9937-572-59-0

Janson typeface with diacritical marks and
Tibetan Classic typeface
Designed and created by Tony Duff
Tibetan Computer Company
http://www.tibet.dk/pktc

Produced, Printed, and Published by
Padma Karpo Translation Committee
P.O. Box 4957
Kathmandu
NEPAL

Committee members for this book: principal translator and composition, Lama Tony Duff; assistant translator, Lama Sergey Dudko; editor, Tom Anderson; graphics, Christopher Duff.

Web-site and e-mail contact through:
http://www.tibet.dk/pktc
or search Padma Karpo Translation Committee on the web.

CONTENTS

INTRODUCTION

This book presents the Great Vehicle sūtra of Śhākyamuni Buddha called *The Noble One Called "Point of Passage Wisdom"*, *A Great Vehicle Sutra.*

The basis for the translation was the Tibetan version of the sūtra obtained from the recently published *Collated Edition of the Tibetan Kangyur* produced by the Chinese Tibetology Research Centre in Beijing and published by them in 2009. Theirs is a particularly useful edition that uses the highly regarded Derge edition of the *Kangyur* or *Translated Buddha Word* as the basis for the edition but shows all variant readings found amongst the eight Tibetan versions of the *Kangyur*—Derge, Yunglo, Lithang, Beijing, Narthang, Chone, Khure, and Zhol. For the sūtra in this book, only a few, minor variations between editions were showing, none of which affected the translation into English. The Tibetan text from their edition has been included in this book, and that is the same in this case as the Derge edition.

The Buddha taught both exoteric and esoteric teachings, the first being summed up under the name "sūtra" and the second under the name "tantra". The sūtra teachings as a whole were later put into three sections—Vinaya, Abhidharma, and Sūtra—and of those, the sūtra here is from the Sūtra section. Moreover, the Buddha taught the sūtra dharma in three steps, each called a turning of the wheel of dharma; the sūtra here is from the third and final turning of the wheel of dharma.

That this sutra is one of the third turning of the wheel sūtras is an important point. The Buddha himself stated in a number of the third turning sūtras that his teaching followed a sequence, with the teachings of the first, second, and third wheels being progressively more profound. He stated clearly in *The Noble One, Unravelling the Intent Sūtra* that the first and second turnings of the wheel were provisional whereas the third teaching was final and definitive. He very clearly states the matter in the *Sūtra Requested by King Dharaṇeshvara* and his explanation, which has become very famous, is known as the "example of cleaning a jewel"; here is the example in its entirety:

> Son of the family, it is like this. For example, there is a skilled jeweller who knows the craft of jewellery well. Of the various types of precious jewel, he has taken a precious jewel which is totally impure. He wets it with a penetrating, chemical salt solution then thoroughly cleans it with a hair cloth and in that way gives it a thorough cleaning. He does not stop his efforts at just that, either. Beyond that, to clean it he wets it with a penetrating decoction then thoroughly cleans it with a woollen flannel and in that way gives it a thorough cleaning. He does not stop his efforts at just that, either. Beyond that, to clean it he also wets it with a strong chemical liquid

then thoroughly cleans it with a fine cotton cloth and in that way thoroughly cleans it. Thoroughly cleansed and free of encrustation, it is now called "an excellent type of Lapis Lazuli".

Son of the family, in the same way, the tathāgata, knowing the element of totally impure sentient beings[1], uses the story of renunciation which is about impermanence, suffering, lack of self, and impurity to arouse disenchantment in those sentient beings who are attracted to cyclic existence and to get them into the taming that goes with the noble dharma. The tathāgata does not stop his efforts at just that much, either. Beyond that, he utilizes the story of emptiness, signlessness, and wishlessness to make them realize the mode of a tathāgata. The tathāgata does not stop his efforts at just that much, either. Beyond that, he utilizes the story of the non-regressing wheel and the story of the total purity of the three spheres to make those sentient beings whose causes vary in nature enter the tathāgata's place.

In the second paragraph, the Buddha says that he taught the dharma in three steps or turnings of the wheel. The first sentence shows the meaning of the first turning of the wheel, the next two show the meaning of the second turning, and the last two show the meaning of the third turning. He makes a

---

[1] Element is a name for the buddha nature. In the third turning of the wheel, beings are classed into three types: buddhas, who are totally pure; those on the path, who are mixed pure and impure; and ordinary beings who are totally impure.

number of points in this paragraph. First, he says that there is a sequence to his teaching and that the third and final turning of the wheel is the penultimate teaching of the sequence. Second, he points out that the second turning of the wheel merely shows the "mode of the tathāgata" whereas the third causes sentient beings of all types "to enter the actual place of the tathāgata", all of which means that the second turning of the wheel shows that a tathāgata is empty whereas the third shows that a tathāgata is not merely empty but is a place that can be entered. Again, the second turning is being put as non-final whereas the third turning is being put as final. Finally, the Buddha uses the words "non-regressing" in relation to the third turning teaching. The meaning of non-regressing in this context is that a person who has understood that non-dual wisdom—which is the essential teaching of the third turning of the wheel—is the definitive and final teaching of the tathāgata, will also understand that a return to a lesser level of teaching—such as the emptiness found in the second turning of the wheel—would be a regression. Hence, that person becomes "non-regressing" as it is called, meaning that he henceforth does not fall back into taking the teachings of either the first or second turnings of the wheel as prime. Henceforth, he stays in the certainty that non-dual wisdom is the ultimate teaching of the Buddha and takes that as the main practice, and does not revert from that certainty and practice to a lesser certainty and practice.

What then is the specific feature of the third turning sūtras that makes them definitive teaching? It is that the Buddha teaches that sentient beings do have "the actual place of the tathāgata"—the tathāgatagarbha—within them and can become buddhas themselves if they access it. The teaching on tathāgatagarbha is somewhat theoretical because it simply teaches that there is a potential for becoming a Buddha. When there is need to teach it in a more practical way, the term sugatagarbha, with the emphasis using that potential to go to enlightenment, is used. In actual fact, the potential for enlightenment is each sentient being's innate wisdom. Therefore, the most profound and also most definitive way of teaching tathāgatagarbha is to point it out as being innate wisdom. The *Point of Passage Wisdom* sūtra is not only a third turning sūtra but one of the third turning sūtras that explicitly teaches tathagatagarbha as wisdom. It is precisely because of this point that we translated the sūtra and made it into this book with explanations of this point.

Importance of the Sutra

There are two reasons for its importance.

It is the condensed version of the Nirvana Sutra

Five of the most important of the Great Vehicle sūtras were known in Tibet as the five "one hundred thousand" sūtras: the *Prajñāpāramitā in One Hundred Thousand Verses* was the one hundred thousand of mind; the *Nirvāṇa Sūtra*, said to contain one hundred thousand testaments of the Buddha, was the hundred thousand of speech; the *Ratnakūṭa Sūtra*, containing the names of one hundred thousand buddhas, was the one hundred thousand of body; the *Avataṃsaka Sūtra*, containing one hundred thousand prayers, was the one hundred thousand of auspiciousness; and the *Descent Into Laṅka Sūtra*, said to possess the methods for subduing one hundred thousand demons, was the one hundred thousand of activity. Each of these grand sūtras was regarded as having a condensed version: for the *Prajñāpāramitā in One Hundred Thousand Verses* it was the *Heart Sūtra,* also called the sūtra of view; for the *Nirvāṇa Sūtra* it was the *Point of Passage Wisdom Sūtra,* also called the sūtra of deeds; for the *Ratnakūṭa Sūtra* it was the *Vajravidāraṇī,* also called the sūtra for washing; for the *Avataṃsaka Sūtra* it was the *Bhadracarīpraṇidhāna,* also called the sūtra of prayers; and for the *Descent into Laṅka Sūtra* it was the *Apattideshana,* also called the sūtra for laying aside evil deeds.

The five condensed versions of the five grand Great Vehicle sūtras, were so important that they were included in the set of "royal sūtras". This set of sūtras was recited by the early Buddhist kings of Tibet—such as King Trisong Deutsan—each day as part of their daily worship.

Thus, the *Point of Passage Wisdom Sūtra* is generally important within the Great Vehicle.

It is one of the profound definitive-meaning sutras

The Buddha taught Other Emptiness in the third turning sūtras and entrusted it to his regent Maitreya, who then taught it to Asaṅga, who wrote those teachings down in the five treatises called *The Five Dharmas of Maitreya.* Tibetan schools that follow the Other Emptiness teaching identify a sub-set of the third turning sūtras which specifically show the profound Other Emptiness meaning.

The sūtras in this set are called, in the writings of the Other Empty system, "the profound definitive-meaning, sūtras[2]" or "the core definitive meaning sutras[3]". They are given this name because, for followers of the Other Empty system, they show the definitive rather than provisional meaning of the Buddha's teaching and they show the most profound level of the Buddha's teaching within the sūtra teachings. Followers of Other Emptiness also call them "the sūtras of the profound meditation system" because of regarding them as the sūtras which show the meaning of the most profound system of view and meditation of the Buddha.

Usually ten sūtras are listed in the set though there also are listings containing fifteen and twenty sūtras. Moreover, the listings made by various Other Emptiness masters are similar but not always exactly the same. Khenpo Tsultrim Gyatso, who follows Jamgon Kongtrul's presentation of the Other Empty teaching, states in his history of the rise of Other Emptiness[4] that the ten sūtras are:

1. *The Sūtra Definitively Teaching the Tathāgata's Great Compassion* contains many chapters, several of which were spoken because of the questions of King Dharaṇeshvara so is also known as *The Sūtra Requested by King Dharaṇeshvara*

---

[2] Tib. nges don zab mo'i mdo.

[3] Tib. nges don snying po'i mdo.

[4] *A Brief Discussion of The Rise of Zhantong Middle Way, Called "The Music of Talk on the Definitive Meaning*, published in *The Other Emptiness, Entering Wisdom beyond Emptiness of Self* by Tony Duff.

The *Point of Passage Wisdom Sūtra* is included in every listing of the sūtras regarded as the ones which show the Other Emptiness meaning. Thus, it is one of a small group of third turning sūtras that forms the backbone of the Other Empty system, a system which is said to be the most profound presentation of the dharma made by the Buddha in his sūtra teachings.

Another sūtra included in every listing is the *Sūtra Petitioned by the Householder Uncouth*. It is a particularly interesting sūtra that focusses on what it means to be a bodhisatva householder. One aspect of the teaching in the sūtra is that it is necessary for a householder to pay attention to non-dual wisdom. This thread runs throughout the sūtra and is the thread that causes it to be included in all the listings. Padma Karpo Translation Committee has translated it because of its importance[5].

---

[5] The sūtra with an extensive explanation of its meaning is published by Padma Karpo Translation Committee under the title *The Sūtra of the Householder Uncouth, A Teaching of the Buddha*
(continued...)

The Teaching Within the Sutra that Supports the Other Empty System

There are two statements in the sūtra that explicitly and un-mistakably show the profound meditation system and thereby support the positions taken by the Other Empty system.

The first statement is:

> All phenomena are luminosity by nature, and that being so, he shall utterly cultivate the perception of no-referencing.

The Buddha has already explained, in the second turning of the wheel of dharma, that all phenomena are empty of a self-nature. Here, he goes further by teaching that, although they are empty of a self-nature, they are not empty of a luminosity nature. Luminosity is the knowing aspect of wisdom, so he is stating in this sūtra that phenomena are in nature wisdom. Moreover, he teaches that the way to cultivate the realization of this view is to engage in non-referencing, that is, to stop engaging in mental, meaning dualistic, mind.

An implication of this teaching is that, although the Buddha's followers might first have to go through the meditation exer-cises of using logic to understand that phenomena are empty, in the end they have to find wisdom by dropping logical

---

[5](...continued)
Showing All-knowing Wisdom and the Householder's Way, translated by Tony Duff, 2013, ISBN 978-9937-572-56-9.

process and simply abiding in non-logical, non-dualistic mind—which is referred to as "wisdom".

The second statement teaches how to find the non-dualistic mind of wisdom and then stay in it:

> If mind is realized, it is wisdom, and that being so,
> he shall utterly cultivate the perception that buddha
> is not to be sought elsewhere.

The versified version of this statement adds something useful:

> Mind is the cause of wisdom's occurrence;
> Do not seek buddha elsewhere!

Wisdom is found in mind and nowhere else. The Buddha taught in the second turning of the wheel that enlightenment is to be sought through logical dissections of the phenomena external to mind. He now teaches that the ultimate way to seek enlightenment is through examination of the mind itself. Realizing mind, meaning realizing the very nature of samsaric mind by seeing it in direct perception, is the cause of, or the doorway to, finding wisdom. Once wisdom has been found, there is nothing to do other than to remain disengaged from the ignorant process of dualistic mind.

The Buddha does not say so in this sūtra, but the details of how to realize the very nature of samsaric mind then stay within non-dualistic wisdom are explained at the sūtra level in the profound meditation system teachings that came down through Maitreya and at the tantra level in the instructions contained in the tantras themselves, for instance, in the in-structions of the ultimate tantric teachings called Mahāmudrā and Mahā Ati.

In that way, the first statement sums up the ultimate view and the second sums up the ultimate meditation as taught by the Buddha. Thus, this very short sūtra contains the essence of the Buddha's final teachings on view and meditation, teachings which are found in both the third turning of the wheel of dharma sūtras and in the fourth turning of the wheel tantras.

Tony Duff
Padma Karpo Translation Committee
Swayambunath,
Nepal,
February 2011

THE NOBLE ONE CALLED "POINT OF PASSAGE WISDOM", A GREAT VEHICLE SUTRA

In Indian Language: ārya ātajñānanāma mahāyāna sūtra
In Tibetan Language: 'phags pa 'da' ka ye shes zhes bya ba
theg pa chen po'i mdo
In English Language: The Noble One Called "Point of
Passage Wisdom", a Great Vehicle Sūtra[6]

I prostrate to all the buddhas and bodhisatvas[7].

---

[6] The original sūtra does not contain the line "In the English ..."
However, if we follow the rules that King Trisong Deutsan set
down by royal decree for the translation of sūtras into the Tibetan language, we must add this line here. We believe that this
is required in the translation of sūtras from Tibetan into other
languages, so we do it here as a model for future translations.

[7] For bodhisatvas, see the glossary.

1

I heard these words at one time. The bhagavan[8] was present in the mansion of the king of gods of Akaniṣhṭha[9], teaching dharma to the retinue and the bodhisatva mahāsattva Ākāshagarbha[10] prostrated to the bhagavan then made a request in these words: "Bhagavan, how should a bodhisatva view the mind of the verge of death?"

The bhagavan instructed:

"Ākāshagarbha, at the point of the time of death, the bodhisatva shall cultivate[11] Point of Passage Wisdom. In regard to

---

[8] "Bhagavan" is an Indian term of respect for someone of high spiritual development. A full discussion of the meaning of the term and an extensive examination of how it should—or should not—be translated can be found in the book *Unending Auspiciousness, The Sutra of the Recollection of the Noble Three Jewels with Commentaries by Ju Mipham, Taranatha, and Tony Duff* by Tony Duff, published by Padma Karpo Translation Committee 2010, ISBN: 978-9937-8386-1-0.

[9] There are a number of places with the name Akaniṣhṭha, some inside saṃsāra and some not. Akaniṣhṭha here is the name of one of the highest levels of the formless realm of saṃsāra.

[10] Ākāshagarbha is the name of one of the eight bodhisatva mahāsattvas who were the heart disciples of Shākyamuni Buddha. Bodhisatva is the general name for someone on the bodhisatva path. Bodhisatva mahāsattva is a name given only to the bodhisatvas of the eighth, ninth, and tenth bodhisatva levels.

[11] The word "cultivate" throughout is the same word as is commonly translated as "meditate". The original term means to cultivate something with the mind. Using cultivate here more
(continued...)

that, the Point of Passage Wisdom is as follows: all phenomena are completely pure by nature, and that being so, he shall utterly cultivate the perception of absence of things[12]. All phenomena are contained within enlightenment mind[13], and that being so, he shall utterly cultivate the perception of great compassion. All phenomena are luminosity by nature, and that being so, he shall utterly cultivate the perception of no-referencing[14]. All things are impermanent, and that being so, he shall utterly cultivate the perception of no attachment to anything. If mind is realized, it is wisdom, and that being so, he shall utterly cultivate the perception that buddha is not to be sought elsewhere."

Putting it in verse, the bhagavan instructed:

> Dharmas are by nature completely pure, so
> He will cultivate the perception of absence of
>   things.
> They are fully possessed by enlightenment mind, so
> He will cultivate the perception of great
>   compassion.
> Dharmas are by nature luminosity, so
> He will cultivate the perception of absence of
>   referencing.

---

[11](...continued)
accurately reflects the Buddha's intent than would using meditate.

[12] "Things", both here and below, has a specific meaning. A "thing" is what conceptual mind believes to be a thing.

[13] For enlightenment mind, see the glossary.

[14] For referencing, see the glossary.

All dharmas are impermanent, so
He will cultivate the perception of absence of
    attachment.
Mind is the cause of wisdom's occurrence;
Do not seek buddha elsewhere!

The bhagavan instructed in those words and the whole retinue of the bodhisatva Ākāshagarbha and the others rejoiced
with delight, then openly praised the teaching of the bhagavan.

The Noble One called "Point of Passage Wisdom", a Great
Vehicle Sutra, is finished.

*The names of the translators who rendered a sūtra from Indian
language into Tibetan language were are usually listed at the end
of the sutra, but not in this case. It was translated from the Tibetan
language into the English language by Lotsāwas Tony Duff and
Sergey Dudko. It was finalized by Tony Duff.*

GLOSSARY OF TERMS

Bodhichitta: see under enlightenment mind.

Bodhisatva: Note that, despite the common appearance of "bodhisattva" in Western books on Buddhism, the Tibetan tradition has steadfastly maintained since the time of the earliest translations that the correct spelling is bodhisatva. In support of this, experts such as Dilgo Khyentse Rinpoche have proclaimed that "bodhisatva" is the correct spelling and explained the reasons for it. A bodhisatva is a person who has engendered the bodhichitta, enlightenment mind, and who has undertaken the path to the enlightenment of a truly complete buddha specifically for the welfare of other beings.

Complete purity, rnam dag: This term refers to the quality of a buddha's mind, which is completely pure compared to a sentient being's mind. The mind of a being in saṃsāra has its primordially pure nature covered over by the muck of dualistic mind. If the being practises correctly, the impurity can be removed and mind can be returned to its original state of complete purity.

Enlightenment mind, Skt. bodhichitta, Tib. byang chub sems: This is a key term of the Great Vehicle. It is the type of mind that is connected not with the lesser enlightenment of an arhat but the enlightenment of a truly complete buddha. As such, it is a mind which is connected with the aim of bringing all sentient beings to that same level of buddhahood. A person who has this mind has entered the Great Vehicle and is either a bodhisatva or a buddha.

It is important to understand that "enlightenment mind" is used to refer equally to the minds of all levels of bodhisatva on the path to buddhahood and to the mind of a buddha who has completed the path. Therefore, it is not "mind striving for enlightenment" as is so often translated but "enlightenment mind", meaning that kind of mind which is connected with the full enlightenment of a truly complete buddha and which is present in all those who belong to the Great Vehicle.

Luminosity, Skt. prabhāsvara, Tib. 'od gsal ba: The core of mind has two aspects: an emptiness factor and a knowing factor. The Buddha and many Indian religious teachers used "luminosity" as a metaphor for the knowing quality of the core of mind. If in English we would say "Mind has a knowing quality", the teachers of ancient India would say, "Mind has an illuminative quality; it is like a source of light which illuminates what it knows".

This term has been translated as "clear light" but that is a mistake that comes from not understanding the etymology of the word. It does not refer to a light that has the quality of clearness (something that makes no sense, actually!) but to the illuminative property which is the nature of the empty mind.

Mind, Skt. chitta, Tib. sems: There are several terms for mind in the Buddhist tradition, each with its own, specific meaning. This term is the most general term for the samsaric type of mind. It refers to the type of mind that is produced because of fundamental ignorance of enlightened mind. Whereas the wisdom of enlightened mind lacks all complexity and knows in a non-dualistic way, this mind of un-enlightenment is a very complicated apparatus that only ever knows in a dualistic way.

Realization, Tib. rtogs pa: Realization has a very specific meaning: it refers to correct knowledge that has been gained in such a way that the knowledge does not abate. There are two important points here. Firstly, realization is not absolute. It refers to the removal of obscurations, one at a time. Each time that a practitioner removes an obscuration, he gains a realization because of it. Therefore, there are as many levels of realization as there are obscurations. Maitreya, in the *Ornament of Manifest Realizations*, shows how the removal of the various obscurations that go with each of the three realms of samsaric existence produces realization.

Secondly, realization is stable or, as the Tibetan wording says, "unchanging". As Guru Rinpoche pointed out, "Intellectual knowledge is like a patch, it drops away; experiences on the path are temporary, they evaporate like mist; realization is unchanging".

Referencing, Tib. dmigs pa: This is the name for the process in which dualistic mind references an actual object by using a conceptual token instead of the actual object. The term referencing implies the presence of dualistic mind and the term non-referencing or without reference implies the presence of non-dualistic wisdom.

Wisdom, Skt. jñāna, Tib. ye shes: This is a fruition term that refers to the kind of mind, the kind of knower possessed by a buddha. Sentient beings do have this kind of knower but it is covered over by a very complex apparatus for knowing, dualistic mind. If they practise the path to buddhahood, they will leave behind their obscuration and return to having this kind of knower.

The Sanskrit term has the sense of knowing in the most simple and immediate way. This sort of knowing is present at the core of every being's mind. Therefore, the Tibetans called it "the particular type of awareness which is there primordially". Because of the Tibetan wording it has often been called "primordial wisdom" in English translations, but that goes too far; it is just "wisdom" in the sense of the most fundamental knowing possible.

ABOUT THE AUTHOR,
PADMA KARPO TRANSLATION COMMITTEE,
AND THEIR SUPPORTS FOR STUDY

I have been encouraged over the years by all of my teachers to pass on the knowledge I have accumulated in a lifetime dedicated to study and practice, primarily in the Tibetan tradition of Buddhism. On the one hand, they have encouraged me to teach. On the other, they are concerned that, while many general books on Buddhism have been and are being published, there are few books that present the actual texts of the tradition. Therefore they, together with a number of major figures in the Buddhist book publishing world, have also encouraged me to translate and publish high quality translations of individual texts of the tradition.

My teachers always remark with great appreciation on the extraordinary amount of teaching that I have heard in this life. It allows for highly informed, accurate translations of a sort not usually seen. Briefly, I spent the 1970's studying, practising, then teaching the Gelugpa system at Chenrezig Institute, Australia, where I was a founding member and also the first Australian to be ordained as a monk in the Tibetan Buddhist tradition. In 1980, I moved to the United States to study at the feet of the Vidyadhara Chogyam Trungpa Rinpoche. I stayed in his Vajradhatu community, now called Shambhala, where I studied and practised all the Karma Kagyu, Nyingma, and Shambhala teachings being presented there and was a senior member of the Nalanda Translation Committee. After the vidyadhara's nirvana, I moved in 1992 to Nepal, where I have been continuously involved with the study, practise, translation, and teaching of the Kagyu system and especially of the Nyingma system of Great Completion. In recent years, I have spent extended times in Tibet with the greatest living Tibetan masters of Great Completion, receiving very pure transmissions of the ultimate levels of this teaching directly in Tibetan and practising them there in retreat. In that way, I have studied and practised extensively not in one Tibetan tradition as is usually done, but in three of the four Tibetan traditions—Gelug, Kagyu, and Nyingma, and also in the Theravada tradition, too.

Padma Karpo Translation Committee (PKTC) was set up to provide a home for the translation and publication work. The committee focusses on producing books containing the best of Tibetan literature, and, especially, books that meet the needs of practitioners. At the time of writing, PKTC has published a wide range of books that, collectively, make a complete program of study for those practising Tibetan Buddhism, and especially for those interested in the higher tantras. All in all, you will find many books both free and for sale on the PKTC web-site. Most are available both as paper editions and e-books.

It would take up too much space here to present an extensive guide to our books and how they can be used as the basis for a study program. However, a guide of that sort is available on the PKTC web-site, whose address is on the copyright page of this book and we recommend that you read it to see how this book fits into the overall scheme of PKTC publications. In short, this is a sutra and one of the sutras which shows Other Emptiness. Therefore, other PKTC publications of sutras to read in conjunction with it are:

- *Maitreya's Sūtras and Prayer, with Commentary by Padma Karpo*, which presents two sūtras petitioned by Maitreya and his famous prayer, and a commentary to the prayer by Padma Karpo;
- *The Noble One Petitioned by the Householder Uncouth, A Great Vehicle Sutra*, another sūtra of the ten profound essence sūtras of Other Emptiness of the third turning of the wheel.

Other books about Other Emptiness are:

- *The Other Emptiness, Entering Wisdom Beyond Emptiness of Self*, a major and exceptionally complete exposition of Other Emptiness with many Tibetan texts and teachings included;
- *Instructions for Practising the View of Other Emptiness*, a text by the first Jamgon Kongtrul showing the practice of Other Emptiness according to the Jonang tradition;
- *The Lion's Roar that Proclaims Zhantong*, a text by Ju Mipham which shows the view of Other Emptiness then goes through arguments raised by Tsongkhapa's followers against the Other Emptiness system;

- *Maitripa's Writings on the View*, a selection of important texts written by the Indian master Maitrīpa showing his understanding of the Other Emptiness approach;

- *A Juggernaut of the Non-Dual View, Ultimate Teachings of the Second Drukchen, Gyalwang Je*, a set of sixty-six teachings on the non-dual view of the tantras which shows clearly the Other Emptiness view of the Kagyus.

- *The Theory and Practice Of Other Emptiness Taught Through Milarepa's Songs*, explanations of Other Emptiness based on two songs of Milarepa— *Authentic Expression of the View of the Middle Way* and *Ultimate View, Meditation, Conduct, and Fruition* showing both the view and meditation of Other Emptiness.

We make a point of including the relevant Tibetan texts in Tibetan script in our books. We also make them available in electronic editions that can be downloaded free from our web-site, as discussed below. The Tibetan text for this book is included at the back of the book and is available for download from our web-site.

Electronic Resources

PKTC has developed a complete range of electronic tools to facilitate the study and translation of Tibetan texts. For many years now, this software has been a prime resource for Tibetan Buddhist centres throughout the world, including in Tibet itself. It is available through the PKTC web-site.

The wordprocessor TibetDoc has the only complete set of tools for creating, correcting, and formatting Tibetan text according to the norms of the Tibetan language. It can also be used to make texts with mixed Tibetan and English or other languages. Extremely high quality Tibetan fonts, based on the forms of Tibetan calligraphy learned from old masters from pre-Communist Chinese Tibet, are also available. Because of their excellence, these typefaces have achieved a legendary status amongst Tibetans.

TibetDoc is used to prepare electronic editions of Tibetan texts in the PKTC text input office in Asia. Tibetan texts are often corrupt so the input texts are carefully corrected prior to distribution. After that, they are made available through the PKTC web-site. These electronic texts are not careless productions like so many of the Tibetan texts found on the web, but are highly reliable editions useful to non-scholars and scholars alike. Some of the larger collections of these texts are for purchase, but most are available for free download.

The electronic texts can be read, searched, and even made into an electronic library using either TibetDoc or our other software, TibetD Reader. Like TibetDoc, TibetD Reader is advanced software with many capabilities made specifically to meet the needs of reading and researching Tibetan texts. PKTC software is for purchase but we make a free version of TibetD Reader available for free download on the PKTC web-site.

A key feature of TibetDoc and Tibet Reader is that Tibetan terms in texts can be looked up on the spot using PKTC's electronic dictionaries. PKTC also has several electronic dictionaries—some Tibetan-Tibetan and some Tibetan-English—and a number of other reference works. The *Illuminator Tibetan-English Dictionary* is renowned for its completeness and accuracy.

This combination of software, texts, reference works, and dictionaries that work together seamlessly has become famous over the years. It has been the basis of many, large publishing projects within the Tibetan Buddhist community around the world for over thirty years and is popular amongst all those needing to work with Tibetan language or deepen their understanding of Buddhism through Tibetan texts.

TIBETAN TEXT

༄༅། །འཕགས་པ་འདའ་ཀ་ཡེ་ཤེས་ཞེས་བྱ་བ་ཐེག་པ་ཆེན་པོ་མདོ།།

༄༅། །རྒྱ་གར་སྐད་དུ། ཨཱརྱ་ཨཱཏྱཛྙཱ་ན་ནཱ་མ་མ་ཧཱ་ཡཱ་ན་སཱུ་ཏྲ། བོད་སྐད་དུ། འཕགས་པ་འདའ་ཀ་ཡེ་ཤེས་ཞེས་བྱ་བ་ཐེག་པ་ཆེན་པོ་མདོ། སངས་རྒྱས་དང་བྱང་ཆུབ་སེམས་དཔའ་ཐམས་ཅད་ལ་ཕྱག་འཚལ་ལོ། །འདི་སྐད་བདག་གིས་ཐོས་པ་དུས་གཅིག་ན། བཅོམ་ལྡན་འདས་འོག་མིན་གྱི་ རྒྱལ་པོའི་ཁང་བཟངས་ན་བཞུགས་ཏེ་འཁོར་ཐམས་ཅད་ལ་ཆོས་སྟོན་པ་དང་། བྱང་ཆུབ་སེམས་དཔའ་སེམས་དཔའ་ཆེན་པོ་ནམ་མཁའི་སྙིང་པོས་བཅོམ་ལྡན་ འདས་ལ་ཕྱག་འཚལ་ནས་འདི་སྐད་ཅེས་གསོལ་ཏོ། བཅོམ་ལྡན་འདས་བྱང་ ཆུབ་སེམས་དཔའ་རྣམ་འཆི་ཁ་མའི་སེམས་ཇེ་ལྟར་བལྟ་བར་བགྱི། བཅོམ་ ལྡན་འདས་ཀྱིས་བཀའ་སྩལ་པ། ནམ་མཁའི་སྙིང་པོ་བྱང་ཆུབ་སེམས་དཔའ་ རྣམ་འཆི་བའི་དུས་ཀྱི་ཚེ་འདའ་ཀ་ཡེ་ཤེས་བསྒོམ་པར་བྱའོ། དེ་ལ་འདའ་ཀ་ ཡེ་ཤེས་ནི་ཆོས་ཐམས་ཅད་རང་བཞིན་གྱིས་རྣམ་པར་དག་པས་ན་དངོས་པོ་མེད་ པའི་འདུ་ཤེས་རབ་ཏུ་བསྒོམ་པར་བྱའོ། ཆོས་ཐམས་ཅད་བྱང་ཆུབ་ཀྱི་སེམས་ སུ་འདུས་པས་ན་སྙིང་རྗེ་ཆེན་པོའི་འདུ་ཤེས་རབ་ཏུ་བསྒོམ་པར་བྱའོ། ཆོས་

15

ཐབས་ཅད་རང་བཞིན་གྱིས་འོད་གསལ་བས་ན་མི་དམིགས་པའི་འདུ་ཤེས་རབ་ཏུ་

བསྐོམ་པར་བྱའོ། །དངོས་པོ་ཐམས་ཅད་མི་རྟག་པས་ན་ཙེ་ལ་ཡང་མི་ཆགས་

པའི་འདུ་ཤེས་རབ་ཏུ་བསྐོམ་པར་བྱའོ། །སེམས་རྟོགས་ན་ཡེ་ཤེས་ཡིན་པས་

ན་སངས་རྒྱས་གཞན་དུ་མི་བཙལ་བའི་འདུ་ཤེས་རབ་ཏུ་བསྐོམ་པར་བྱའོ། །

བཅོམ་ལྡན་འདས་ཀྱིས་ཚིགས་སུ་བཅད་དེ་བཀའ་སྩལ་པ། ཆོས་རྣམས་རང་

བཞིན་རྣམ་དག་པས། །དངོས་པོ་མེད་པའི་འདུ་ཤེས་བསྐོམ། །བྱང་ཆུབ་

སེམས་དང་རབ་ལྡན་པས། །སྐྱིང་རྗེ་ཆེན་པོའི་འདུ་ཤེས་བསྐོམ། །ཆོས་

རྣམས་རང་བཞིན་འོད་གསལ་བས། །དམིགས་པ་མེད་པའི་འདུ་ཤེས་

བསྐོམ། །དངོས་པོ་ཐམས་ཅད་མི་རྟག་པས། །ཆགས་པ་མེད་པའི་འདུ་

ཤེས་བསྐོམ། །སེམས་ནི་ཡེ་ཤེས་འབྱུང་བའི་རྒྱུ། །སངས་རྒྱས་གཞན་དུ་

མ་ཚོལ་ཅིག །བཅོམ་ལྡན་འདས་ཀྱིས་དེ་སྐད་ཅེས་བཀའ་སྩལ་པ་དང་། །

བྱང་ཆུབ་སེམས་དཔའ་རྣམ་མཁའི་སྙིང་པོ་ལ་སོགས་པའི་འཁོར་འདུས་པ་

ཐམས་ཅད་རབ་ཏུ་དགའ་མགུ་ཡི་རངས་ནས། བཅོམ་ལྡན་འདས་ཀྱིས་

གསུངས་པ་ལ་མངོན་པར་བསྟོད་དོ།། །།འཕགས་པ་འདའ་ཀ་ཡེ་ཤེས་

ཞེས་བྱ་བ་ཐེག་པ་ཆེན་པོ་མདོ་རྫོགས་སོ།། ॥

INDEX

www.ingramcontent.com/pod-product-compliance
Lightning Source LLC
Chambersburg PA
CBHW020943100426
42741CB00006BA/844